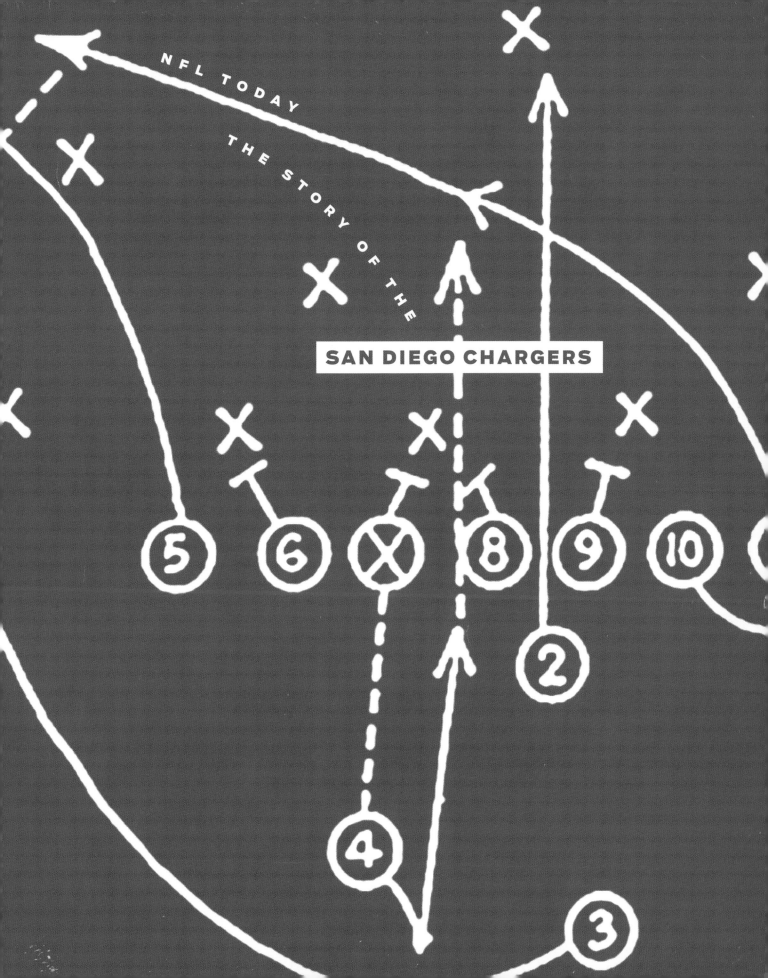

NFL TODAY

THE STORY OF THE

SAN DIEGO CHARGERS

NFL TODAY

THE STORY OF THE SAN DIEGO CHARGERS

JIM WHITING

CREATIVE EDUCATION

PUBLISHED BY CREATIVE EDUCATION
P.O. BOX 227, MANKATO, MINNESOTA 56002
CREATIVE EDUCATION IS AN IMPRINT OF THE CREATIVE COMPANY
WWW.THECREATIVECOMPANY.US

DESIGN AND PRODUCTION BY BLUE DESIGN
ART DIRECTION BY RITA MARSHALL
PRINTED IN THE UNITED STATES OF AMERICA

PHOTOGRAPHS BY AP IMAGES, GETTY IMAGES (KC
ALFRED/UNION-TRIBUNE, AL BELLO, BRUCE BENNETT
STUDIOS, DAVE CROSS/NFL, DAVID DRAPKIN,
STEPHEN DUNN, STEPHEN DUNN/ALLSPORT, GIN
ELLIS, FOCUS ON SPORT, GEORGE GOJKOVICH, JEFF
HAYNES/AFP, HARRY HOW, WALTER IOOSS JR./SPORTS
ILLUSTRATED, PAUL JASIENSKI, GENE LOWER/NFL,
JIM MCISAAC, AL MESSERSCHMIDT, DONALD MIRALLE,
RONALD C. MODRA/SPORTS IMAGERY, NFL PHOTOS,
DARRYL NORENBERG/NFL, DOUG PENSINGER, ROGERS
PHOTO ARCHIVE, PAUL SPINELLI, RICK STEWART,
GREG TROTT, CHARLES AQUA VIVA/NFL, STUART
WESTMORLAND, MARILYNN YOUNG/AFP)

COPYRIGHT © 2014 CREATIVE EDUCATION

LIBRARY OF CONGRESS CATALOGING-IN-PUBLICATION DATA
WHITING, JIM.
THE STORY OF THE SAN DIEGO CHARGERS / BY JIM WHITING.
P. CM. — (NFL TODAY)
INCLUDES INDEX.
SUMMARY: THE HISTORY OF THE NATIONAL FOOTBALL LEAGUE'S
SAN DIEGO CHARGERS, SURVEYING THE FRANCHISE'S BIGGEST
STARS AND MOST MEMORABLE MOMENTS FROM ITS INAUGURAL
SEASON IN 1960 TO TODAY.
ISBN 978-1-60818-318-0
1. SAN DIEGO CHARGERS (FOOTBALL TEAM)—HISTORY—JUVENILE
LITERATURE. I. TITLE.

GV956.S29W45 2013
796.332'6409794985—DC23   2012033816

FIRST EDITION
9 8 7 6 5 4 3 2 1

COVER: RUNNING BACK RYAN MATHEWS
PAGE 2: QUARTERBACK PHILIP RIVERS
PAGES 4—5: DEFENSIVE END IGOR OLSHANSKY
PAGE 6: FULLBACK LORENZO NEAL

TABLE OF CONTENTS

SIDELINE STORIES

MEET THE CHARGERS

THE CITY OF SAN DIEGO, CALIFORNIA, SITS ALONG THE PACIFIC OCEAN

Charging from the Gate

When Spanish explorer Juan Rodriguez Cabrillo splashed ashore in San Diego Bay in 1542, he was the first European to set foot on the west coast of the United States. More than 200 years later, San Diego became the first European settlement in present-day California. Although blessed with one of the world's most appealing climates, the city's development was relatively slow. That changed during and after World War II, when its extensive natural harbor and proximity to the Pacific Theater spurred the establishment and growth of numerous military facilities. Today, San Diego is the second-largest city in California and eighth-largest in the U.S. It is also the home of one of the most colorful and exciting franchises in the National Football League (NFL), the San Diego Chargers.

The Chargers were formed in Los Angeles in 1959 as a member of the new American

COACH SID GILLMAN, RECEIVER LANCE ALWORTH, AND QUARTERBACK JOHN HADL

Sid Gillman

COACH / CHARGERS SEASONS: 1960–69, 1971

In the very first College versus Pros All-Star Game in 1934, a young player named Sid Gillman had a revelation. After Bronko Nagurski of the Chicago Bears laid a punishing hit on him, Gillman realized that he could have a longer and healthier career as a coach than as a player. In an era when the running game was the bread and butter of any offense, Gillman was convinced of the big-play possibilities of a high-powered passing attack. By implementing his high-scoring passing strategies, he led the Chargers to five divisional crowns in the AFL's first six seasons and won the AFL championship in 1963. The league was forced to adapt to his style of play just to compete with the Chargers. "The Chargers' image of the lightning bolt was perfect for Sid Gillman and how his teams played football," said Alex Spanos, who took ownership of the Chargers in the 1980s. Gillman was innovative in his use of game film as a method of preparing his team for its next matchup. He was also the first head coach to win divisional titles in both the AFL and the NFL.

JOHN HADL QUARTERBACKED THE CHARGERS (AS BACKUP THEN STARTER) FOR 11 SEASONS

Football League (AFL). The club's owner was Barron Hilton, son of hotel mogul Conrad Hilton. Through a public "name-the-team" contest, the name "Chargers" was suggested. Hilton approved. "I liked it because they were yelling 'charge' and sounding the bugle at Dodgers Stadium and at USC [University of Southern California] games," he said.

Befitting a team with a lightning-bolt logo, the Chargers immediately electrified their fans. Coach Sid Gillman had previously won an NFL championship with the Los Angeles Rams. With a talented roster featuring running back Paul Lowe and quarterback Jack Kemp, the Chargers went 10–4 in 1960 and won the AFL's Western Division. Although they lost to the Houston Oilers in the AFL Championship Game, the good times were just beginning. Those good times would not be in Los Angeles, though. L.A. fans weren't charged up about the new team. So, in 1961, Hilton took the team to San Diego.

In San Diego, the Chargers surrounded Lowe and Kemp with more talent by drafting running back Keith Lincoln and defensive linemen Earl Faison and Ernie Ladd. These players carried the Chargers to

"That's what kept pro football in San Diego."

COACH SID GILLMAN
ON JACK MURPHY

another Western Division title in 1961. Unfortunately, the Oilers again topped the Chargers in the AFL Championship Game.

Looking for a boost to push them to the top, the Chargers traded for quick, sure-handed receiver Lance Alworth in 1962. In 1963, Alworth—nicknamed "Bambi" because of his deerlike grace and energy—gave the team that boost by posting 1,205 receiving yards and scoring 11 touchdowns. With Alworth and two new quarterbacks, veteran Tobin Rote and youngster John Hadl, sparking the AFL's most explosive passing attack, San Diego won its division again.

San Diego fans rejoiced as the Chargers won their first AFL championship, demolishing the Boston Patriots 51–10. The Chargers' offense was nearly unstoppable, and Lincoln blasted through the Patriots' defense for 206 rushing yards. "This isn't a football team," said Boston's awestruck coach, Mike Holovak. "It's a machine."

The Chargers machine continued to operate at full throttle in 1964 and 1965 as San Diego returned to the AFL Championship Game, only to lose to the Buffalo Bills both times. Alworth and Hadl continued their offensive heroics, but the departure of Ladd in 1965 and Faison in 1966 hurt the team. Over the next three seasons, San Diego put together mediocre records, though fans thrilled to the play of defensive back and kick returner Leslie "Speedy" Duncan. Duncan, regarded as one of the best kickoff return men in AFL history, lived up to his nickname in a 1967 game when he became one of just a handful of professional players ever to return an interception and a fumble for touchdowns in the same game.

In 1970, the AFL and NFL merged, beginning a new era in professional football. In their 10 AFL seasons, the Chargers won 5 division titles and 1 league championship. But the team had grown old. Even the greats now failed to put up great numbers. Alworth's production dropped off, and Hadl completed fewer than half of his passes. Late in the 1971 season, Gillman stepped down as head coach.

Power of the Press

San Diego sportswriter Jack Murphy heard that Chargers owner Barron Hilton was thinking about relocating the team because of poor attendance in Los Angeles in the team's inaugural season in 1960. Despite unfavorable economic conditions and a lack of big-time sports in his own city, Murphy used his column in the *San Diego Union* to urge fans to pledge money to buy tickets if the team moved there. Hundreds of pledges rolled in, and Hilton was convinced. "Without Jack Murphy, I never would've moved the franchise," Hilton later said. "Jack was very perceptive in foreseeing that San Diego was a major-league city, that a pro football franchise would succeed there." Even after the Chargers had moved to San Diego, Murphy wasn't done. He urged his fellow citizens to vote for a new stadium. Former coach Sid Gillman said, "That's what kept pro football in San Diego." The facility was named for Murphy soon after his death in 1980, making it the only stadium named for a sportswriter. Although it was renamed Qualcomm Stadium in 1997, the playing field itself still bears Murphy's name.

IN JANUARY 1988, JACK MURPHY STADIUM PLAYED HOST TO SUPER BOWL XXII

DAN FOUTS MAY HAVE STARTED SLOWLY, BUT HE BECAME A HALL-OF-FAMER IN 1993

San Diego general manager Harland Svare took over as coach, and the team began to rebuild. Within 1 year, Svare made 21 trades. In 1973, the Chargers brought in veteran quarterback Johnny Unitas to replace the traded Hadl, but Unitas was no better. Rookie quarterback Dan Fouts took over, but he threw a high volume of interceptions, and the 1973 Chargers finished a woeful 2–11–1.

n 1974, Tommy Prothro took over as the Chargers' head coach. The team sported a new look, trading its old white helmets for blue ones. Despite these changes, the team's play remained poor. Fouts continued to struggle, and San Diego strung together losing seasons through 1976. Yet the team continued to believe in Fouts. That trust would soon pay off.

Lance Alworth

WIDE RECEIVER / CHARGERS SEASONS: 1962–70 / HEIGHT: 6 FEET / WEIGHT: 184 POUNDS

Some football players succeed with hard work and determination. Others, such as Lance Alworth, seem to be born stars, possessing rare natural speed and grace. Recognizing that the San Diego Chargers needed a deep threat on offense in the early 1960s, assistant coach Al Davis tenaciously pushed for the Chargers to acquire the services of Alworth, who was drafted by the AFL's Oakland Raiders in 1962. Chargers management listened and soon swung a trade to bring Alworth to San Diego. In the early years of the AFL, the Chargers were a team that embraced a fast-paced, crowd-pleasing brand of football, and Alworth was at the center of that excitement. The receiver known as "Bambi" was a constant big-play threat. In 9 years with the Chargers, he averaged more than 1,000 yards per season. "Lance Alworth was one of maybe three players in my lifetime who had what I would call 'it'," said Davis. "You could see right from the beginning that he was going to be a superstar." In 1978, Alworth became the first AFL player to be enshrined in the Pro Football Hall of Fame.

The Chargers Score a Title

After the 1963 season, a tie in the AFL's Eastern Division prompted a special playoff matchup between the Boston Patriots and the Buffalo Bills. Boston won the game easily and traveled to Balboa Stadium in San Diego to take on the Chargers in the AFL Championship Game. The Chargers had been in the big game twice before—as the Los Angeles Chargers in the very first AFL title game and again in 1961 after moving to San Diego—but had come up short both times. The "Bolts" started the scoring in the 1963 title game with a touchdown run by quarterback Tobin Rote. Boston had made its way to the championship game with a much-heralded defense, but the Chargers quickly proved that they could score at will. Running back Keith Lincoln led the way with 329 yards in total offense and 2 touchdowns. By game's end, the Chargers had drubbed the Patriots 51–10 for their first championship. Although they would approach championship heights several times afterward, that 1963 triumph remains the Chargers' only league title.

Flying with Air Coryell

In 1978, the Chargers achieved their first winning season (9–7) of the decade. Early in that season, San Diego fans saw their team fall victim to one of the most infamous episodes in franchise history: the Oakland Raiders' "Holy Roller" play. Trailing the Chargers 20–14 with just 10 seconds left in the fourth quarter, the Raiders intentionally and repeatedly fumbled the ball forward until they could fall on it in the end zone to win the game. The play infuriated Chargers fans and players and led to an NFL rule change limiting the offense's ability to advance a fumble on fourth down or in a game's final two minutes. Thanks in part to that defeat, San Diego started the season 1–4. But after Don Coryell stepped in as the club's new head coach in midseason, the Chargers surged to seven victories in their final eight games.

Coryell deserved much of the credit for the Chargers' sudden success. So did Fouts. In 1979,

JOHN JEFFERSON WAS ONE OF THE NFL'S TOP WIDE RECEIVERS OF THE LATE 1970s

Dan Fouts

QUARTERBACK / CHARGERS SEASONS: 1973–87 / HEIGHT: 6-FOOT-3 / WEIGHT: 204 POUNDS

A football team that loves to throw the deep ball needs a quarterback with a big arm, intelligence, and the toughness to take a hit. The San Diego Chargers found all those attributes in Dan Fouts. While he lacked great running speed, Fouts excelled at standing in the pocket and reading the field. And when he found his target, he would deliver a tight spiral with his powerful right arm. The Chargers' high-powered offense of the late 1970s and early '80s was called "Air Coryell" after the coach who designed the passing plays, but Fouts was the engine that made it work. The Chargers went from a mediocre football team to a perennial contender, winning the AFC West in 1979, 1980, and 1981. The longtime Chargers quarterback was a six-time Pro-Bowler, a two-time All-Pro, and winner of the NFL Most Valuable Player (MVP) award in 1982. Ernie Zampese, the team's offensive coordinator during the Air Coryell era, knew he had something special in his quarterback, saying, "Dan Fouts had a tremendous ability to focus, unlike anyone else I've ever seen, and he was an unbelievable leader."

the seventh-year quarterback finally emerged as a genuine star, setting a new NFL single-season record by passing for 4,082 yards. He helped propel the Chargers to a 12–4 record and the American Football Conference (AFC) West Division championship—their first division title since 1965. With Fouts leading Coryell's brilliant pass-oriented offense, sportswriters began calling the Chargers' attack "Air Coryell."

San Diego began to look like the Chargers of old. From 1979 to 1981, the team won the AFC West title every year and posted a combined 33–15 record. Fouts just seemed to get better. In 1981, the quarterback who many considered the toughest in the NFL broke his own single-season passing record for the second straight year, throwing for a whopping 4,802 yards and 33 touchdowns.

nfortunately, the biggest prize of all eluded the Chargers, who could never quite reach the Super Bowl. In 1981, the team lost in the AFC Championship Game for the second straight season, despite a loaded roster that included Pro Bowl defensive linemen Gary "Big Hands" Johnson, Louie Kelcher, and Fred Dean. "I can't tell you how much it hurts to come this far and lose two years in a row," Coach Coryell said after the 1981 title game loss to the Cincinnati Bengals.

The Chargers made the playoffs again in 1982, only to fall to the Miami Dolphins in the second round. The team's defense was dealt a terrible blow after the season when Johnson, Kelcher, and Dean all departed. The Chargers then slipped into a losing slump that would last most of the 1980s.

As injuries began to slow down Fouts, receiver Charlie Joiner remained one of the team's few consistent bright spots. At 5-foot-11 and 185 pounds, Joiner was rather small by NFL standards, but he made up for it with a powerful mixture of instincts and toughness. Joiner posted four 1,000-yard seasons during an amazing 18-season NFL career. Before he finally retired after the 1986 season at the age of 39, he would catch 750 passes for 12,146 yards—both NFL records. Although the Chargers of the '80s

San Diego Disco

Many sports teams have a fight song. Usually they are short, simple, and designed to pump up the crowd. They are not usually disco! During the mid-1970s, Chargers owner Gene Klein watched his team struggle on the field and at the ticket office. By 1980, Klein decided that drastic measures were necessary to inject some life into his struggling franchise. He launched a multimedia campaign, complete with a new slogan, T-shirts, decals, and a new Chargers theme song, "San Diego Super Chargers." As the team gained success on the field, the disco-flavored song kept fans singing in the stands every time the Chargers put points on the board. More than three decades later, the song, recorded by Captain Q.B. and the Big Boys, remains as popular as ever—except with opposing teams. "I hate that song," said New England Patriots head coach Bill Belichick. "It means it's not going well for us." Chargers fans, however, love belting out such lyrics as, "With high voltage play, we won't let up a minute, we're going all the way—all the way!"

SAN DIEGO FANS GET CHARGED UP DURING A GAME AND ROOT FOR THEIR FAVORITE PLAYERS

KELLEN WINSLOW SR. PASSED ALONG HIS TIGHT END SKILLS TO HIS SON AND NAMESAKE

DON CORYELL RAN HIS SUCCESSFUL OFFENSE IN SAN DIEGO FOR 9 SEASONS

featured other outstanding targets—including tight end Kellen Winslow and receivers John Jefferson and Wes Chandler—the constant link was Joiner. "I don't recall him ever missing a practice at all since I've been in San Diego," Coryell said. "One time, he cracked a rib and didn't take a day off. He said, 'I'll work through it.'"

Except for the efforts of Joiner and his fellow receivers, the mid-1980s were dark seasons in San Diego. In 1986, the team found a new defensive star as rookie end Leslie O'Neal netted 12.5 quarterback sacks to win the NFL Defensive Rookie of the Year award. He would go on to a career that featured six Pro Bowl appearances. The Chargers started 8–1 a year later but stumbled down the stretch and missed the playoffs again. Fouts and Winslow then retired.

After finishing dead last in the AFC West in 1989, San Diego hired a new general manager to ignite the "Bolts" again: Bobby Beathard. Widely considered one of the NFL's smartest minds, Beathard had rebuilt the Washington Redskins a decade earlier. Chargers management hoped he would work similar magic in San Diego.

The Epic in Miami

Some football games are played so well by both teams that it seems wrong that either team should lose. The 1982 playoff game between the Chargers and the Miami Dolphins was one such game, an epic battle remembered as one of the best in NFL history. After the Chargers jumped out to a first-quarter 24–0 lead, the Dolphins inserted backup quarterback Don Strock and used a trick "hook and lateral" play to score just before halftime, bringing the score to 24–17. The second half found the two teams in a 38–38 tie as the Dolphins lined up for a last-second, 43-yard field goal to win the game. But San Diego tight end Kellen Winslow, who was battling injuries and dehydration, blocked the attempt. In overtime, kicker Rolf Benirschke finally hit a 29-yard field goal to give the Chargers the victory. The exhausting "Epic in Miami" set a number of NFL playoff records, including most combined points (79), most combined yards (1,036), and most combined passing yards (836). It was also 1 of just 7 pro games in which both quarterbacks passed for more than 400 yards.

ROLF BENIRSCHKE KICKED IN THE CHARGERS' FIRST AND LAST SCORES IN THE EPIC GAME

The Bolts Rebuild

Beathard quickly proved his genius by selecting linebacker Junior Seau with San Diego's top pick in the 1990 NFL Draft. An incredibly powerful player who could bench-press 500 pounds, Seau became an instant terror in the NFL as the heart of San Diego's defense. Bill Belichick, the head coach of the Cleveland Browns, was astounded by the Chargers' new star. "Junior Seau is the best defensive player we've faced, I'd say, by a pretty good margin," said Belichick.

After San Diego posted losing records in 1990 and 1991, Beathard hired Bobby Ross, who had led Georgia Tech University to the 1990 national college championship, as head coach in 1992. Beathard then picked up a new quarterback by signing former Redskins signal-caller Stan Humphries. With these new pieces in place, the Chargers made a startling comeback, winning their first AFC West title in more than a decade with an 11–5 record.

The team slipped to 8–8 in 1993, as Humphries missed part of the season with an injury. The Chargers added a new weapon that year in rookie running back Natrone

NATRONE MEANS WOULD GO ON TO BECOME A CONSISTENT YARD GAINER FOR THE BOLTS

✕ Charlie Joiner

WIDE RECEIVER / CHARGERS SEASONS: 1976–86 / HEIGHT: 5-FOOT-11 / WEIGHT: 188 POUNDS

Charlie Joiner was drafted as a defensive back in 1969 by the Houston Oilers, but after playing briefly on defense and special teams, Joiner switched to offense as a wide receiver. When he was traded to the Chargers in 1976, he realized his true potential and became a star. He was a crucial part of the Chargers' run to the AFC Championship Game in 1981 and playoff charge in 1982. Joiner combined his physical gifts with precise route running and a head for the game that made him a consistent playmaker. He was a smart and unassuming player who preferred to make his mark on the field rather than by talking. As quarterback Dan Fouts piloted the Chargers' offense, Joiner was usually his first, and best, target. San Francisco 49ers coaching legend Bill Walsh once called Joiner "the smartest, the most calculating receiver the game has ever known." In January 2008, the Chargers hired Joiner as their wide receivers coach, hoping he would pass some of his wisdom along to the team's receiving corps.

**49ERS COACH BILL WALSH
ON CHARLIE JOINER**

Means, who helped the team go 11–5. San Diego beat the Dolphins and a heavily favored Pittsburgh Steelers team in two thrilling playoff games to win the AFC championship and then headed to Miami for its first Super Bowl. "We were very much underdogs," Humphries later said of San Diego's playoff run. "Pittsburgh was doing their Super Bowl videos already, getting ready for that. You kind of go into the game and just let it all go and know you've got nothing to lose." The Chargers would fall one win short of an NFL championship, though, losing to the San Francisco 49ers by a score of 49–26.

The Chargers returned to the playoffs in 1995, but the year ended in disappointment with a 35–20 loss to the Indianapolis Colts. Seau and such players as receiver Tony Martin continued to shine, but it wasn't enough. The Bolts went 8–8 in 1996, then crashed to the AFC West cellar again, finishing the 1997 season 4–12.

Beathard traded two veteran players and what amounted to two seasons' worth of draft choices to the Arizona Cardinals for the right to the second overall pick in the 1998 NFL Draft. San Diego used the pick to select Ryan Leaf, a 6-foot-5 quarterback out of Washington State University. Hoping that Leaf would lead the team forward after adjusting to the pro game, the Chargers and their fans waited … and waited. Leaf never emerged as the star the team needed, and the Chargers continued to fade. After an embarrassing 2000 season in which the team went 1–15 and Leaf alienated teammates and the media with temper tantrums and immature behavior, San Diego released him.

After churning through three coaches in four rocky seasons, San Diego hired veteran coach Marty Schottenheimer in 2002. Although the Chargers had gone just 5–11 the year before, Schottenheimer inherited a team with potential. In the 2001 NFL Draft, the Chargers had used the fifth overall pick to grab LaDainian Tomlinson, a shifty and highly touted running back out of Texas Christian University. They had also drafted a tough young quarterback named Drew Brees.

Behind the leadership of Coach Schottenheimer and the great play of Tomlinson—who rushed for 1,683 yards—the 2002 Chargers proved that they were no longer pushovers, going 8–8. Although the San Diego faithful were saddened when 12-time Pro-Bowler Junior Seau left town after the season, they were encouraged by Tomlinson's emergence as one of the NFL's most dangerous ballcarriers. "I've never coached a running back that has the kind of explosive change of direction he's got," Schottenheimer said. "He's got the ability to see things and make cuts that a lot of the winning running backs in this league don't have." The veteran coach and the new running back would need a little time, but they would soon have the Chargers flying high.

The Bolts dropped their first five games in 2003 and continued to struggle,

JUNIOR SEAU'S PASSIONATE PLAY EVENTUALLY LEFT HIM WITH TRAUMATIC BRAIN DAMAGE

Saving the Season

San Diego linebacker Dennis Gibson was not having a good game against Pittsburgh in the AFC Championship Game on January 15, 1995. The man he was defending on a pass play scored a first-quarter Steelers touchdown. Another missed coverage put the ball on the Chargers' 9-yard line with less than two minutes remaining and the Chargers clinging to 17–13 lead. Then Gibson dropped a pass that would have been a game-ending interception. On fourth down, Steelers quarterback Neil O'Donnell threw toward running back Barry Foster. But Gibson lunged to his right and swatted the ball away with his left hand, and the Chargers were Super Bowl–bound for the first time. "When Gibby made the play, I just went up to him and said, 'Hey, that's it,'" said safety Stanley Richard. "'Let's party!'" Many Chargers fans believe it is the franchise's all-time greatest single play and call it the "Immaculate Deflection." The nickname is a play on the Steelers' famous 1972 "Immaculate Reception," when running back Franco Harris snagged a deflected pass on the game's final play and raced into the end zone for a miraculous, game-winning score.

DENNIS GIBSON HAD HIS MOMENT IN THE SUN WITH THE "IMMACULATE DEFLECTION"

LaDAINIAN TOMLINSON SET MANY RECORDS UNDER COACH MARTY'S WATCH

finishing the season a dismal 4–12. The silver lining to the dark cloud of that season was earning the number-one overall pick in the 2004 NFL Draft. However, San Diego's top choice, quarterback Eli Manning, declared that he would not play for the Chargers, forcing them to trade him to the New York Giants for the fourth overall pick—quarterback Philip Rivers—plus future draft picks.

fter scoring just 38 touchdowns in 2003, the Chargers came alive in a big way in 2004, finding the end zone 55 times. Brees had an exceptional year with 27 touchdown passes, and Tomlinson continued to cement his standing as arguably the game's best running back with 18 touchdowns. Additionally, a new offensive weapon emerged in tight end Antonio Gates. Largely dedicated to basketball in college, Gates signed as an undrafted free agent and put his size and natural athleticism to use in becoming a big-play threat. Coach Schottenheimer admitted that the Chargers struck gold through dumb luck. "If we had known he was going to be that good, we would have picked him number one instead of signing him as a free agent," he said.

In 2004, San Diego used its new offensive firepower to win the AFC West for the first time since 1994. The celebration was short-lived, though, as the New York Jets took care of the Chargers in the playoffs, earning a 20–17 victory in overtime.

ANTONIO GATES HAD SCORED 83 TOUCHDOWNS FOR SAN DIEGO BY 2013

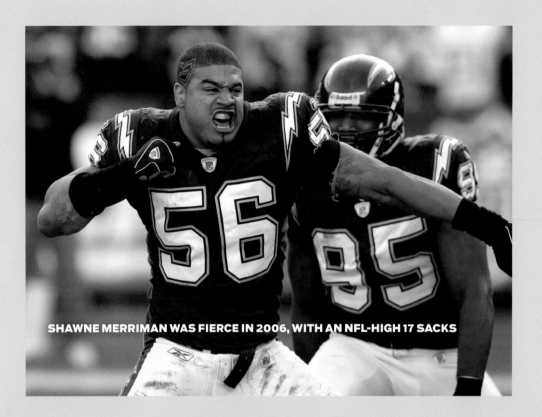

SHAWNE MERRIMAN WAS FIERCE IN 2006, WITH AN NFL-HIGH 17 SACKS

Knocking at the Door

Injuries and a tough schedule held the Chargers in check in 2005, and they finished third in their division with a 9–7 record. However, another star emerged that season. Rookie linebacker Shawne Merriman delivered plenty of crushing tackles, recorded 10 sacks, and won NFL Defensive Rookie of the Year honors. After the season, the Chargers faced a tough decision. Brees was a free agent and expected big money. But he had also suffered a shoulder injury in one of the last games of the season. With the younger Rivers waiting in the wings, the Chargers released Brees.

With Rivers under center and Tomlinson continuing to run wild, the team finished 2006 with a franchise-best 14–2 record. In the playoffs, the Chargers took a 14–10 first-half lead over the powerful New England Patriots. With eight and a half minutes to go in the fourth quarter, San Diego still held a 21–13 lead. An interception by Chargers defensive back Marlon McCree appeared likely to seal a San Diego victory, but the ball was stripped away and recovered by the Patriots. New England then seized the

PHILIP RIVERS HAD SOME OF HIS BEST STATISTICAL SEASONS AFTER 2007

Junior Seau

LINEBACKER / CHARGERS SEASONS: 1990–2002 / HEIGHT: 6-FOOT-3 / WEIGHT: 248 POUNDS

Like the lightning bolt on his helmet, Junior Seau moved fast and struck hard. Nicknamed "The Tasmanian Devil," Seau played with remarkable energy and a nose for the ball. He was a superb all-around defender who was able to rush the quarterback, chase down ballcarriers from sideline to sideline, and even drop back into pass coverage. While Chargers fans adored their hard-hitting linebacker for his relentless hustle and flair for the game, the fist-pumping "lightning bolt dance" Seau sometimes showcased to celebrate big plays didn't always go over so well with opponents. He soon abandoned his notorious dance but continued to wreak havoc on opposing offenses, becoming one of only four players since the 1970 NFL-AFL merger to appear in 12 straight Pro Bowls. In San Diego's Super Bowl appearance after the 1994 season, he tallied 11 tackles and 1 sack. His energy and leadership on the field affected the whole team. Sadly, after retiring from the game, an emotionally troubled Seau took his own life in 2012. "He brought something to the game that very few people have brought to the game," said former Chargers general manager Bobby Beathard. "He made people around him better."

momentum, tying the game and then taking the lead. Minutes later, a missed 54-yard field goal sent the Chargers to a 24–21 defeat—one of the most devastating playoff losses in team history. Rivers later said, "When I think back to the 14–2 season [in 2006] when we had the home playoff game and got beat, you wonder if it was a little too big for us."

Frustrated by its postseason near misses, San Diego made the controversial decision to fire Coach Schottenheimer in the off-season and hire veteran coach Norv Turner. The team struggled early in 2007, but the midseason pickup of wide receiver Chris Chambers and the emergence of third-year receiver Vincent Jackson helped the Chargers finish with an 11–5 record, tops in the AFC West once again.

IN OCTOBER 2009, NORV TURNER PASSED THE 100-LOSS MARK

After defeating the Tennessee Titans and Indianapolis Colts, the Chargers had a chance to take revenge on the Patriots in the AFC Championship Game. But once again, the Patriots were too powerful, sending the Chargers home by a score of 21–12.

That loss seemed to take the wind out of San Diego's sails. While players such as Rivers, Gates, and speedy cornerback Antonio Cromartie gave some fine performances in 2008, Tomlinson appeared to have lost a step, and the club dropped several painfully close games as it started 4–8. Refusing to quit, though, the Chargers won their last four games to recapture their division, then won a playoff game over the Colts before their season finally ended.

The following year, injuries to key players caused San Diego to limp to a 2–3 start. Then, suddenly, all systems were go as the Chargers ran off 11 wins in a row. Rivers led the way, passing for more than 4,000 yards and 28 touchdowns. Unfortunately, the good times ground to a halt in the playoffs. Kicker Nate Kaeding missed three field goal attempts as the Chargers dropped a 17–14 decision to the Jets. Soon afterward, the team released Tomlinson.

Hoping to replace Tomlinson and give Rivers some offensive support, the Chargers traded up in the NFL Draft to select speedy Fresno State running back Ryan Mathews. The team hoped that Mathews and bullish veteran Mike Tolbert would give the Chargers a potent and well-balanced ground game.

One of a Kind

Fans expected a low-scoring game when the Chargers played the Steelers in Pittsburgh on November 16, 2008. Snow flurries were flying, the field was slick, and temperatures were frigid. San Diego struck first on LaDainian Tomlinson's three-yard touchdown run. Quarterback Philip Rivers was sacked for a Steelers safety early in the second quarter, and Pittsburgh kicker Jeff Reed booted a 21-yard field goal as time expired in the half. Reed connected on a 41-yarder midway through the third quarter for an 8–7 Steelers lead. San Diego countered with a 22-yard Nate Kaeding field goal with less than seven minutes left, and Reed closed out the scoring with a 32-yard effort with 15 seconds remaining to complete the very first 11–10 score in more than 13,000 NFL games. "It was an awesome baseball game … an unbelievable baseball game," joked Pittsburgh safety Ryan Clark. The score was very nearly a mundane 17–10. On the final play, Pittsburgh safety Troy Polamalu scooped up what seemed to be an errant Chargers lateral and raced into the end zone. After review, however, officials ruled it had been an illegal forward pass, and the one-of-a-kind 11–10 tally stood.

FIELD CONDITIONS WERE NOT IDEAL FOR THE LOW-SCORING 2008 AFFAIR

PLAYERS ENTER AND EXIT QUALCOMM STADIUM THROUGH TUNNELS OFF THE FIELD

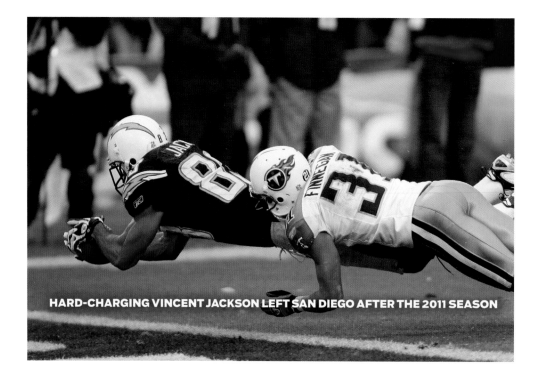
HARD-CHARGING VINCENT JACKSON LEFT SAN DIEGO AFTER THE 2011 SEASON

The Chargers continued to be slow out of the gate in 2010, starting the season just 2–5. This time, they couldn't recover, finishing 9–7 and out of the playoffs for the first time in four years. They also achieved a dubious distinction: even though San Diego was just the eighth NFL team ever to lead the league in both total offense and total defense, it became the only team besides the 1953 Philadelphia Eagles to rank tops in both categories without making the postseason. In the end, a spectacular season by Rivers—who threw for more than 4,700 yards—went to waste.

After a promising 4–1 start to the 2011 campaign, the Chargers lost six games in a row in especially frustrating fashion, with all but one defeat coming by a touchdown or less. With Mathews churning out 1,091 rushing yards on the year, the Bolts rebounded to win four of their final five and finish in a three-way tie for the top spot in the AFC West with Denver and Oakland. Only the Broncos, though, made the playoffs by virtue of a better record among common opponents.

Boasting an offense that was one of the highest-scoring in the league, the Chargers used the off-season to try to tighten up their defense. To that end, San Diego selected linebacker Melvin Ingram, defensive end Kendall Reyes, and strong safety Brandon Taylor with their top three picks in the 2012 NFL Draft. "Shoddy defense helped lead to San Diego's failure to reach the playoffs last year," noted one draft analyst, "so the addition of three players that could wind up as starters ranks as a fine haul for a team that doesn't usually have much trouble scoring points."

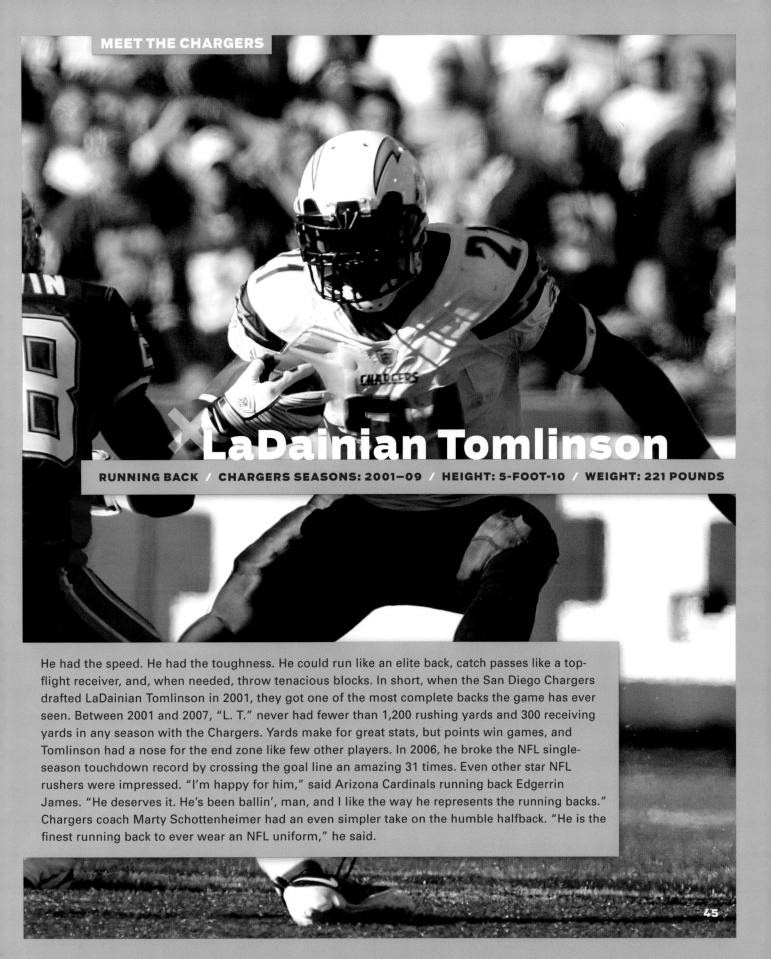

LaDainian Tomlinson

RUNNING BACK / CHARGERS SEASONS: 2001–09 / HEIGHT: 5-FOOT-10 / WEIGHT: 221 POUNDS

He had the speed. He had the toughness. He could run like an elite back, catch passes like a top-flight receiver, and, when needed, throw tenacious blocks. In short, when the San Diego Chargers drafted LaDainian Tomlinson in 2001, they got one of the most complete backs the game has ever seen. Between 2001 and 2007, "L. T." never had fewer than 1,200 rushing yards and 300 receiving yards in any season with the Chargers. Yards make for great stats, but points win games, and Tomlinson had a nose for the end zone like few other players. In 2006, he broke the NFL single-season touchdown record by crossing the goal line an amazing 31 times. Even other star NFL rushers were impressed. "I'm happy for him," said Arizona Cardinals running back Edgerrin James. "He deserves it. He's been ballin', man, and I like the way he represents the running backs." Chargers coach Marty Schottenheimer had an even simpler take on the humble halfback. "He is the finest running back to ever wear an NFL uniform," he said.

FOLLOWING HIS 2011 BREAKTHROUGH, RYAN MATHEWS WAS NAMED TO THE PRO BOWL

AS OF 2013, TAKEO SPIKES HAD NEVER PARTICIPATED IN A PLAYOFF GAME

Although none of the three new recruits were starters in 2012—and though Taylor suffered a torn ACL near the end of the season—San Diego believed that all three would become major contributors. In the meantime, the Bolts' season could be summed up in three words: peak (a 3–1 start), valley (losing 7 of 8 games), peak (a 3–1 finish). The result was an overall 7–9 record, their first losing season since 2003 and the third year in a row that San Diego missed the playoffs. Coach Turner was fired in favor of Denver Broncos offensive coordinator Mike McCoy, who had famously overseen the emergence of rookie phenom Tim Tebow. "They all laughed at me when I walked in yesterday with this big ol' bag with all these books and binders and everything," McCoy said. "Well, that's my life's work. We've got a detailed plan that [general manager] Tom [Tedesco] and I are going to put together.... There's going to be some changes." Broncos wide receiver Brandon Stokley provided a ringing endorsement of McCoy, whose appointment in San Diego was his first as a head man: "I think he's going to be a great head coach. Very detail-oriented, knows the game, relates with players very well."

San Diego has long been regarded as one of the most colorful and exciting teams in the NFL, especially on the offensive side of the ball. In the last decade, the Chargers have come oh-so-close many times to making a Super Bowl run, only to fall just short. Yet optimism runs high in San Diego, one of the sunniest cities in America, and fans remain confident that their beloved Bolts will soon charge to the ultimate football glory.

X INDEX